All About
Flowers

Claire Throp

Raintree

Raintree is an imprint of Capstone Global Library Limited, a company incorporated in England and Wales having its registered office at 7 Pilgrim Street, London, EC4V 6LB – Registered company number: 6695582

www.raintreepublishers.co.uk
myorders@raintreepublishers.co.uk

Edited by Claire Throp and Brynn Baker
Designed by Peggie Carley
Picture research by Ruth Blair
Production by Victoria Fitzgerald
Originated by Capstone Global Library Ltd
Printed and bound in China by RR Donnelley Asia

ISBN 978 1 406 28437 9
18 17 16 15 14
10 9 8 7 6 5 4 3 2 1

British Library Cataloguing in Publication Data
A full catalogue record for this book is available from the British Library.

Acknowledgements
We would like to thank the following for permission to reproduce photographs: Getty Images: Andrew Dernie, cover; iStockphoto: srebrina, 9 (left); Shutterstock: Anna Omelchenko, 12, 23 (middle), Artens, 9 (right), Birdiegal, 20 (left), Butterfly Hunter, 20 (right), Charles Brutlag, 22, Eduardo Ramirez Sanchez, 21, Elena Elisseeva, 8, Filipe B. Varela, 5, Frank L. Junior, 14, freya-photographer, 13, Habitus, 19, Jorge Salcedo, 16, Kenneth Keifer, 17, Kostex, 11, loreanto, 15, 23 (top), Pavelk, 6, Sompoch Tangthai, back cover, 18, Stefan Holm, 4, Yevgeniy Steshkin, 10, 23 (bottom), Yuriy Kulik, 7

We would like to thank Michael Bright for his invaluable help in the preparation of this book.

Every effort has been made to contact copyright holders of material reproduced in this book. Any omissions will be rectified in subsequent printings if notice is given to the publisher.

Contents

What are plants? 4

What do plants need to grow? . . . 6

What are flowers? 8

Petals 12

Shapes 16

Flowers as food 20

Plants need flowers 22

Picture glossary 23

Index 24

Notes for parents and teachers . . 24

What are plants?

Plants are living things.

flower

stem

leaf

root

seed

Plants have
many parts.

What do plants need to grow?

Plants need water to grow.

Plants need sunlight
and air to grow.

What are flowers?

Many plants grow flowers.

Some plants have one flower.
Some plants have lots of flowers.

Flowers make **seeds**.

New plants grow from seeds.

Petals

petal

A **petal** is one part of a flower.

Some flowers have purple petals.

Some flowers have red petals.

Some flowers have **patterns**
on their petals.

Shapes

Flowers can be different shapes.
Some flowers look like a ball.

Some flowers look like a heart.

Some flowers look like a star.

Some flowers look like a bell.

Flowers as food

Hummingbirds and butterflies
get food from flowers.

Bees get food from flowers.

Plants need flowers

seed

Flowers make seeds. Seeds grow
and become new plants.

Picture glossary

 **pattern** colours, shapes, or lines that are repeated

 **petal** part of a flower that is often bright in colour

 **seed** part of a plant that new plants grow from

Index

air 7

bees 21

butterflies 20

food 20, 21

hummingbirds 20

leaves 5

patterns 15

petals 12, 13, 14, 15

roots 5

seeds 5, 10, 11, 22

shapes 16, 17, 18, 19

stems 5

sunlight 7

water 6

Notes for parents and teachers

Before reading

Gather together a variety of flowers or photos of flowers. Ask children to describe each, including its colour and shape. If you have actual flowers, ask children to smell them. Ask children why they think flowers smell and why some have colourful patterns. (to attract insects and some birds)

After reading

- Ask children why insects and birds are neccessary for plants to survive. How do insects and birds help plants?

- Ask children to draw a flower from the book and label the flower's parts, such as the petals, roots, and stem.

- Ask children to work with partners to describe the flowers in the book. One child describes the flower's colour, pattern, or shape, and the other child finds the flower in the book. Then the children switch roles.